Deborah Kovacs

Noises in the Night

The Habits of Bats

STECK-VAUGHN
ELEMENTARY · SECONDARY · ADULT · LIBRARY

A Harcourt Company

www.steck-vaughn.com

This book is dedicated to wildlife researchers who work in the world's endangered forests.

Steck-Vaughn Company

First published 2001 by Raintree Steck-Vaughn Publishers, an imprint of Steck-Vaughn Company.

Copyright © 2001 Turnstone Publishing Group, Inc.
Copyright © 2001, text, by Deborah Kovacs

ISBN 0-7398-2472-4

For information about this and other Turnstone reference books and educational materials, visit Turnstone Publishing Group on the World Wide Web at http://www.turnstonepub.com.

Photo credits listed on page 48 constitute part of this copyright page.

Printed and bound in the United States of America.

1 2 3 4 5 6 7 8 9 0 LB 05 04 03 02 01 00

Contents

1 Noises in the Night

The cries of the howler monkey (above) are so loud that they often surprise visitors to Barro Colorado Island. This kind of monkey grows quiet in the evening.

Night falls on the **rain forest** of Barro Colorado Island. The bright blue of the daytime sky fades and turns to violet. Barro Colorado Island is part of **Panama**. It is located in the southernmost part of Central America.

Day creatures creep, crawl, or fly to their nests, burrows, and roosts. Screeching jungle birds grow

silent. The howler monkey's bellow is so loud by day that it seems to shake the trees. But it is quiet now. Its cry is replaced by the sound of the tungara frog—*Tuuunnnn-ga-ra-chuck!*—and the scratchy calls of insects called katydids. Other insects called cicadas add a deafening buzz, like the sound of a power saw.

Now the forest belongs to the creatures of the night. They come out to search for food and for others of their own kind. They move in the safety of darkness. Spiders crawl to the edge of a small stream. Their tiny eyes glow bright green in reflected light. Flowers open. Their scents tell the insects and other forest creatures that nectar, or sweet liquid, is there for the taking. And hungry bats leave their day roosts, or resting places. They dart through the air, looking for food.

(above)
As night falls, some animals awaken, like these tent-making bats.

(below)
Some creatures, like this rain forest spider, are only active at night.

5

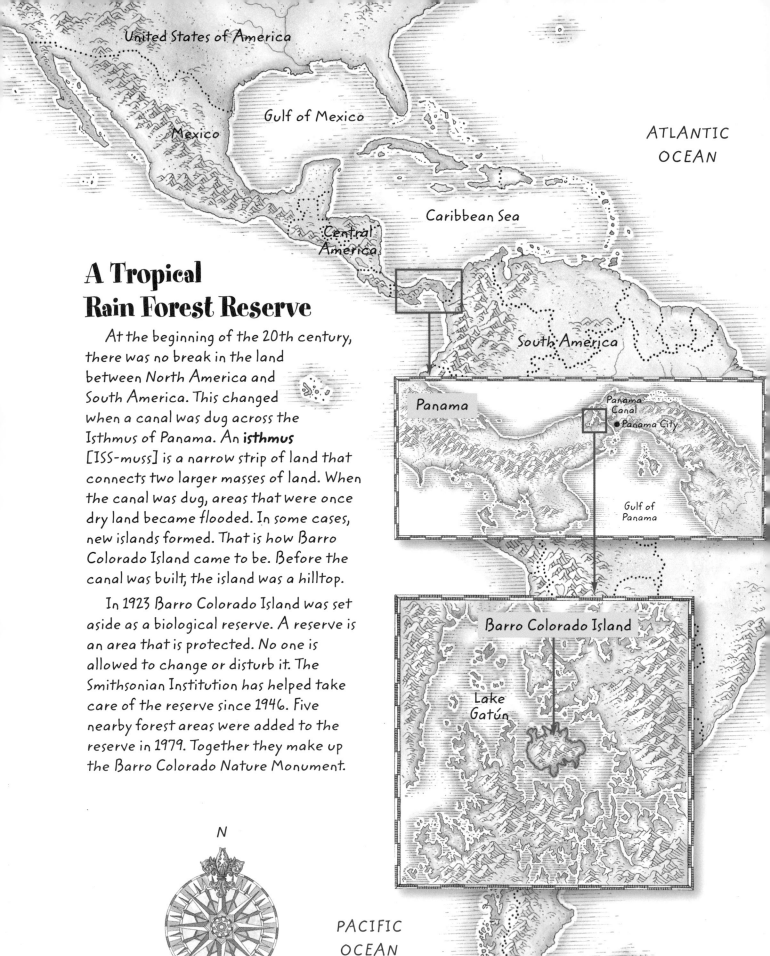

A Tropical Rain Forest Reserve

At the beginning of the 20th century, there was no break in the land between North America and South America. This changed when a canal was dug across the Isthmus of Panama. An **isthmus** [ISS-muss] is a narrow strip of land that connects two larger masses of land. When the canal was dug, areas that were once dry land became flooded. In some cases, new islands formed. That is how Barro Colorado Island came to be. Before the canal was built, the island was a hilltop.

In 1923 Barro Colorado Island was set aside as a biological reserve. A reserve is an area that is protected. No one is allowed to change or disturb it. The Smithsonian Institution has helped take care of the reserve since 1946. Five nearby forest areas were added to the reserve in 1979. Together they make up the Barro Colorado Nature Monument.

United States of America

Gulf of Mexico

Mexico

ATLANTIC OCEAN

Caribbean Sea

Central America

South America

Panama

Panama Canal

Panama City

Gulf of Panama

Barro Colorado Island

Lake Gatún

N

PACIFIC OCEAN

Barro Colorado Island is covered with a tropical rain forest. The temperature there is always warm. There are two seasons on the island—wet and dry. The wet season runs from the middle of April to the middle of December. During those months it rains almost every day, and the forest is leafy. The dry season is from mid-December to mid-April. In those months there is hardly any rain. Some trees drop their leaves, many plants flower, and many fruits grow. The two seasons make very good living conditions for a huge number of different kinds of plants and animals.

Barro Colorado Island and some nearby mainland forests form a **nature reserve**. A reserve is an area where plants, animals, and their habitats are protected. The reserve is home to a large variety of **species**. A species is one of the groups used by scientists to classify living things. Members of the same species are able to breed with each other. Their offspring are able to breed, too.

How do the many species on and near Barro Colorado Island manage to live together? How do they find enough to eat and the right kind of place to live? Each species has its own **niche** [NITCH]. A species' niche is its place in the **community**. Each species has its own foods and places to live. Scientists study rain forests like the one on Barro Colorado Island to learn how these niches work.

Rain forests are busy, noisy places. There is life everywhere. It is on every surface, in puddles of water, on rocks, and in holes, like this one that scientist Elisabeth Kalko is inspecting. The air rings with hums, clicks, and screeches. Rain forests cover only six percent of land on Earth, but more than half of Earth's plants and animals live there.

7

Do You Hear What I Hear?

Bats are active at night. Many people think that bats cannot see, but this is not true. Almost all bats can see fairly well. Most bats also have another way to help them find their way in the dark and to locate food. They **echolocate**.

To echolocate, a bat continuously makes sounds as it flies. Then it listens for any echoes. An echo means that the sound the bat made has bounced off an object and has reflected back to the bat.

From an echo, a bat can tell how far away an object is, how big it is, and whether it is moving. A moving object might mean a meal. Echolocation is how this Greater Bulldog Bat finds its meal, an insect.

Some scientists come to Barro Colorado Island to study trees and other plants. Some study insects. Others are interested in different animals, such as birds, mammals, or reptiles. The scientists share data, or information. They want to understand life in the rain forest. Their work helps explain how all the plants and animals there live together.

Research on Barro Colorado Island takes place 24 hours a day. Most scientists work during the day. But some head into the forest as the sun sets. Among these "night owls" are researchers who come to Barro Colorado Island to study bats.

The Night Shift

As the sky darkens, a small team of researchers moves into action. The scientists have been waiting beside a cove, a small, sheltered body of water. They

8

hope to see the Greater Bulldog Bat, a bat that eats fish and insects. They want to photograph the bat as it hunts and record the sounds it makes.

One scientist lifts a **night vision scope**, a special kind of binoculars, to her eyes. She is Elisabeth Kalko of the University of Tübingen in Germany. Elisabeth has spent a lot of time in this forest. She is studying the lives of bats. With the scope, she watches. Several bats begin to swoop and dive over the cove. They are hunting for fish and insects.

Elisabeth sees that one of the bats has the wing shape and flying pattern of the Greater Bulldog Bat. This is the bat that she and the others hoped to find. To be sure, Elisabeth points a microphone toward the bat. She wants to listen to the calls the bat makes as it flies. The calls of Greater Bulldog Bats are very easy for Elisabeth to recognize. "They sound somewhat like *beee beeeeeup, beee beeeup*," she says.

Most of the calls bats make are too soft or too high to be heard by the human ear. Elisabeth's microphone picks up the bat sounds and sends them to a device that the researchers call a "**bat detector**." The detector makes the bat calls sound lower and slower so that humans can hear them. The detector also sends the slowed-down calls to a tape recorder. Researchers can study the tapes later in the lab.

Night vision scope— makes light many times brighter

Bat detector—makes bat calls sound lower and slower

Loudspeaker

Microphone— records bat calls

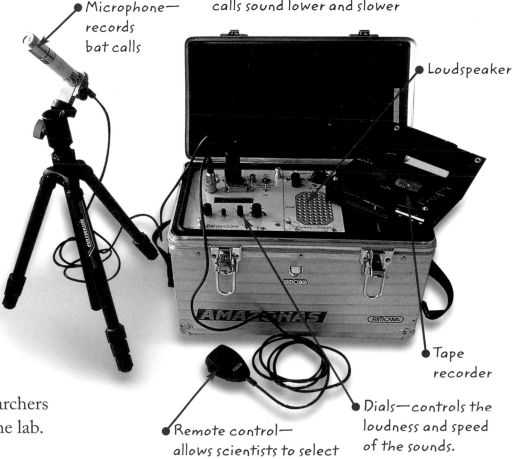

Tape recorder

Dials—controls the loudness and speed of the sounds.

Remote control— allows scientists to select which calls to record.

"Bats are incredibly fast with everything they do," Elisabeth says. For example, when bats echolocate, or use echoes to find **prey**, or food, things happen very quickly. "When bats echolocate, it can sound like a very fast *taka-taka*." Elisabeth listens closely to the slowed-down sounds to be sure she is watching a Greater Bulldog Bat. She wants to take pictures of this bat as it searches for food. She uses a multiflash system, 12 flashes attached to two cameras. Each multiflash image shows many pictures in one. She begins to take pictures, listening even more closely to the bat detector. She listens for a certain set of sounds.

Terminal Buzz

Just before a bat catches prey, its call changes. "The bat has a very special set of sounds it uses when it has found prey and attempts to capture it," says Elisabeth. At that instant, its calls speed up

Say Cheese

One important tool to bat researchers is the **multi-flash camera system,** like the one Elisabeth is operating below. The system has two cameras. Each camera is attached to 12 flashes. The shutters of both cameras stay open while the flashes go off very quickly.

The picture that the system makes is really many pictures in one. The pictures may show a bat capturing its food.

until they sound like buzzes. Researchers call this the "**terminal buzz**." Terminal means end or limit. The calls in the terminal buzz are the last calls a bat makes before capturing its prey. The buzz sends back a huge number of echoes so the bat can locate its prey exactly. The bat detector makes recordings of these buzz calls.

As she listens for the terminal buzz calls, Elisabeth presses the button on the multiflash system over and over. She takes many pictures throughout the night.

The next day, in the laboratory, Elisabeth and others will load the pictures and the sound recordings into a computer. They will work to match the pictures with the sounds the bat was making when the pictures were taken. They will add the information to thousands of other records collected by researchers over many years.

(above)
The ten bats in this picture are really ten pictures of the same bat. It is a Greater Bulldog Bat capturing a fish. Elisabeth took hundreds of pictures to get this one, the one she wanted.

(below)
The Greater Bulldog Bat has a large mouth and wide cheek pouches to store the fish and insects it catches.

Looking at Sound

Sound pictures can help researchers study bat behavior. One kind of sound picture is a sonogram. Sonograms show a sound's pitch, or how high or low the sound is. Pitch is measured in units called kilohertz (kHz). The higher the sound's pitch, the higher the kilohertz. Sonograms also show how long a sound lasts, and how loud the sound is. Time is measured from left to right in thousandths of a second, or milliseconds (ms). Color is used to show the loudness of a sound. Red is loudest. Blue is softest.

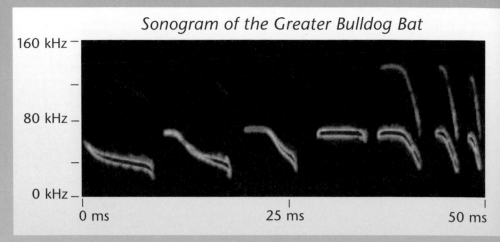

Sonogram of the Greater Bulldog Bat

160 kHz —

80 kHz —

0 kHz —

0 ms   25 ms   50 ms

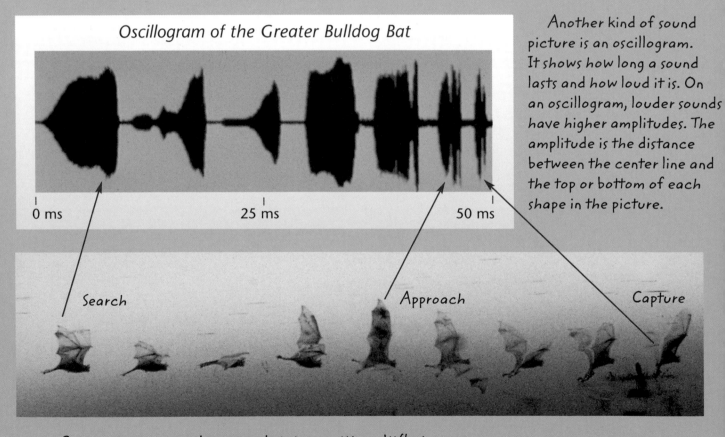

Oscillogram of the Greater Bulldog Bat

0 ms   25 ms   50 ms

Another kind of sound picture is an oscillogram. It shows how long a sound lasts and how loud it is. On an oscillogram, louder sounds have higher amplitudes. The amplitude is the distance between the center line and the top or bottom of each shape in the picture.

Search   Approach   Capture

Bat researchers combine sound pictures with multiflash pictures to learn what the different sounds a bat makes mean. The Greater Bulldog Bat in the multiflash picture makes different sounds at different times—when it looks for fish (search), when it finds a fish (approach), and just before it catches the fish (capture).

Studying Bats

Bat researchers on Barro Colorado Island want to understand how bats live in a tropical rain forest. They want to answer many questions. How many different kinds of bats live here? How many bats are there? Do the kinds of bats change over time? Do bats travel between the protected forests of the island and the nearby mainland? Researchers look for answers to these questions by conducting community studies. These studies have helped researchers find over 70 different kinds of bats on the island and in nearby forests. (There are only about 40 kinds of bats in the United States and Canada.) Each of these kinds of bats belongs to its own species.

Other studies, called single-species studies, help researchers understand one kind of bat. These studies help them know how a bat lives. They learn what a bat eats, where it lives, how it hunts, how it flies, what calls it makes, and how its body is built.

By combining large community studies and smaller single-species studies, researchers have a picture of how the many different kinds of bats on Barro Colorado Island live together. They also can see how the bats live with other animals. In this way, they can understand how bats' niches work.

But each answer raises new questions. "Now that we have a little more knowledge," says Elisabeth, "we can see how little we know. Barro Colorado Island is the ideal place for long-term studies because it is protected. We have a chance to see how things live together and change over time. In other places when you come back, the forest may be gone." By learning about bats, researchers can help protect areas where bats live.

(above)
Elisabeth uses equipment in her lab on Barro Colorado Island to study bat calls.

(below)
Elisabeth often publishes the results of her research in articles like the one below. This way, she can share the results of her work with scientists all over the world.

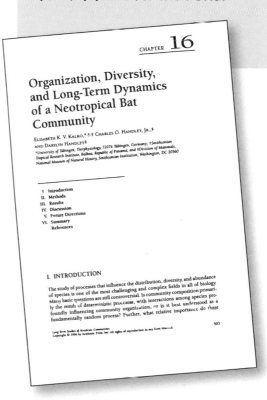

CHAPTER 16

Organization, Diversity, and Long-Term Dynamics of a Neotropical Bat Community

ELISABETH K. V. KALKO,*,†,‡ CHARLES O. HANDLEY, JR.,†
AND DARELYN HANDLEY†
*University of Tübingen, Tierphysiolgy, 72076 Tübingen, Germany; †Smithsonian Tropical Research Institute, Balboa, Republic of Panama; and ‡Division of Mammals, National Museum of Natural History, Smithsonian Institution, Washington, DC 20560

I. Introduction
II. Methods
III. Results
IV. Discussion
V. Future Directions
VI. Summary
    References

I. INTRODUCTION

The study of processes that influence the distribution, diversity, and abundance of species is one of the most challenging and complex fields in all of biology. Many basic questions are still controversial. Is community composition primarily the result of deterministic processes, with interactions among species profoundly influencing community organization, or is it best understood as a fundamentally random process? Further, what relative importance do these

503

Bat Basics

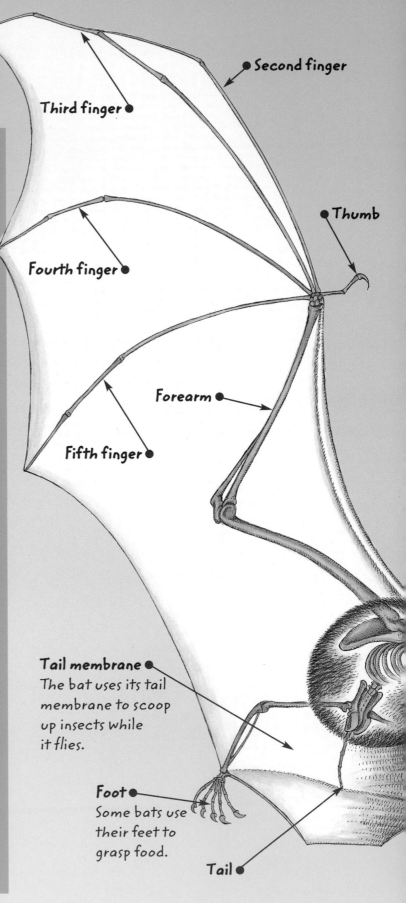

Second finger

Third finger

Fourth finger

Thumb

Fifth finger

Forearm

Bats are **mammals**. This means that mother bats give birth to live young and feed their young with milk. There are more than 900 different kinds of bats. Bats are found on every continent on Earth, but they don't live in polar regions, high mountains, or extreme deserts.

Most bats travel and search for food by flying. Some bats eat insects. Other bats eat fruit, nectar, fish, frogs, and other small animals. Many bats use echolocation to find food, and to find their way safely in the darkness.

Flying foxes, one group of bats, usually do not echolocate. Instead they use good eyesight and a good sense of smell to find the fruit, pollen, flowers, and leaves they eat and the nectar they drink.

Tail membrane The bat uses its tail membrane to scoop up insects while it flies.

Foot Some bats use their feet to grasp food.

Tail

This is a picture of a White-lined Bat, an insect hunter that looks for food at forest edges and gaps.

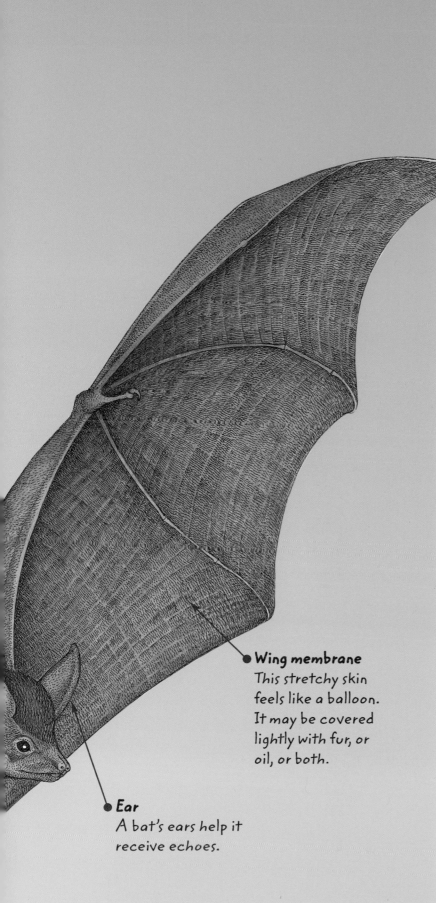

Wing membrane
This stretchy skin feels like a balloon. It may be covered lightly with fur, or oil, or both.

Ear
A bat's ears help it receive echoes.

Almost all bats see in black and white. Some bats can see better than humans in dim light.

A bat uses its powerful chest and back muscles to move its wings.

A bat's wings are so thin that you can see light through them.

The toes of a bat's feet grasp tightly without effort. This lets the bat hang upside down.

2 It's a Jungle Out There

The research station at Barro Colorado Island, shown above, is a very good place to work. Laboratory space, computers, and other equipment are available. Meals are provided. The dormitories, or places where the researchers sleep, are comfortable.

Dietrich von Staden, one of Elisabeth's students, sits in the island's computer lab on a February afternoon. He logs on to the Internet to check the weather for the coming evening. It looks good. The temperature will be around 24°C (75°F). Any rain will be light and will probably fall before sunset.

Dietrich checks all of his equipment. He has 48 poles, 24 nylon nets called "**mist nets**," and 80 small bags. He also has a folding table and chairs, a sheet of plastic, and laundry line. Finally, there are cameras, film, a scale, and a stack of paper.

Dietrich's two student assistants arrive. They load the gear and set off into the forest of Barro Colorado Island. A half-hour later, they arrive at the trunk of a fig tree. It is as tall as a three-story building and one of the largest trees on the island. There they set up the **research site** where they will work through the night.

Each mist net is about 12 meters (about 40 feet) long. The nets are set up across an area that is about 100 to 200 meters wide (about 330 to 650 feet). When the nets are opened, they are about 2 ½ meters (about 8 feet) high. But for now, Dietrich and his assistants keep the mist nets rolled up. They don't want to catch anything before the night begins.

The plastic sheet is stretched between two nearby trees. It will be a shelter for the researchers in case of rain. The table and chairs are set up. About an hour and a half later, the site is ready.

Dietrich takes a look around the site to check that everything is in order. The group walks back to the research station. From about 4 P.M. to 5:30 P.M., the researchers eat their dinner and catch a little sleep. It's going to be a long night.

Once Dietrich and his assistants have set up the mist nets, this spot will look like a jumble of badminton nets. Many different types of bats fly through this part of the forest.

"Batting," or catching bats, usually takes place on dark, moonless nights. When the moon is bright, many bats stay in their roosts. Roosts are caves, hollow trees, or other areas where bats rest during the day. Bats may go without food to avoid being eaten by enemies. A bat's enemies include a screech owl (below) or a boa (above), shown waiting for fruit-eating bats in a tree filled with ripe figs.

All in a Night's Work

The researchers head back into the forest just before sunset. Dietrich usually works at a research site for four nights in a row. On the first two nights, he uses the bat detector to make sound recordings of bats in the area. "Some bats simply don't fly into mist nets," he says. These bats fly too high. "We don't have a chance to catch them unless we can find their roosts, which may be 45 meters (about 140 feet) above the ground." The researchers use the bat detector to hear high-flying bats.

The last two nights at a research site, Dietrich uses mist nets. "If we catch a bat in a mist net, we mark it. Then if we catch it again, we won't count it again. We just note that it has moved to a new location." But Dietrich can't use mist nets for more than two nights in the same place. "I might collect 100 bats in my mist nets the first night," he says.

"The second night, 60. The third night, it's not really worth it." Many kinds of bats are smart. If there is a net somewhere in their neighborhood, they will soon learn to avoid it. However, bats also forget. So, after a few weeks, mist nets can be set up again in the same place. Dietrich visits the

An evening of batting starts just after sunset and lasts until just before sunrise. The researchers open the mist nets and sit down to wait until the bats begin to fly. They are (clockwise from upper left) Gerald Keith, Elisabeth Kalko, Ceinwen Edwards, Dietrich von Staden, and Maria Arrocha.

same sites in a regular pattern. That way, he can see which bats are found at certain places at different times of the year.

As the sun begins to go down, it's time for the bat researchers to start their night of work. They unroll the mist nets in the forest path. Now they wait for the bats to arrive.

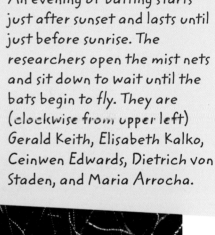

Bats are caught in mist nets because the nets are so thin and light that bats do not sense them until it is too late. This bat will be freed from the net as quickly as possible.

How to Examine a Bat

To free a bat caught in a mist net, Elisabeth holds the bat so that it can't turn its head. Then she frees the bat and puts it in a small canvas "**capture bag.**" The bat moves and cheeps for a few minutes. Then it calms down.

The bagged bats are hung on a line in order from smallest to largest. The smallest bats are usually examined first. They are the most fragile. First, José Rincon weighs the bat in its bag. Another researcher records the weight (❶) on a data sheet like the one on the right.

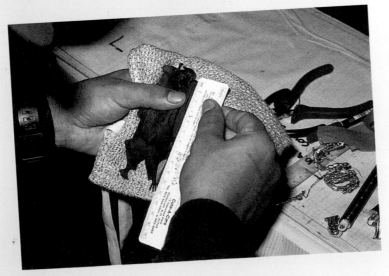

Now the bat is removed from the bag. The **data recorder** makes a note of the kind of bat (❷) and whether it is male or female (❸). The length of the bat's body, the width of its **wingspan**, and the size of other body parts, such as its forearm, are measured and recorded (❹).

The researchers then tell the bat's age by looking at its finger joints (**5**). Joints are where bones meet. A young bat's finger joints are different from those of an older bat. You can see growth plates, places where new bone grows, at the younger bat's joints.

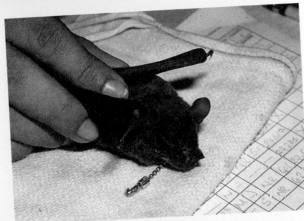

Next, two researchers place a lightweight metal necklace around the bat's neck. This is called marking. The number on the necklace is recorded on the data sheet (**6**). If the bat is captured again, the researchers can compare the records of the different captures.

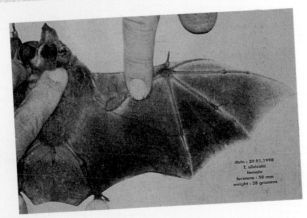

date : 20.01.1998
T. silvicola
female
forearm : 50 mm
weight : 28 gramms

After the bat is marked, a photograph of the bat's wing is taken (**7**). It goes into a file with photographs of the wings of all the other bats that have been captured and examined.

Here is one of Dietrich's data sheets.

capt.hour	net	height shelf	**2** species	**1** weight g	**3** sex	**5** age	repro. status	**4** fore-arm	**6** band #	re-cap	fruit	fae-ces	**7** photo
									28625	X			
									28795		X	fig	
7	2100	13	3	A J	99 - 50 = 49	F	SA	NR	63 28796				5
38	00:44	1	1	Aj	124 - 52 = 72	M	A	6×3	72 10377				
39	0028	12	8	APil	62 - 52 = 10	M	J	NR	38 10378				
40	1240	23	3	A W	64 - 53 = 11	♂	A	NR	43 28797				
41	1239	22	4	Michir	97 - 53 = 44	♂	SA	N.R	63 28798				
42	0005	4	2	A J	71 - 54 = 17	♂	A	6×3	43				
			3	CP					28696	X			

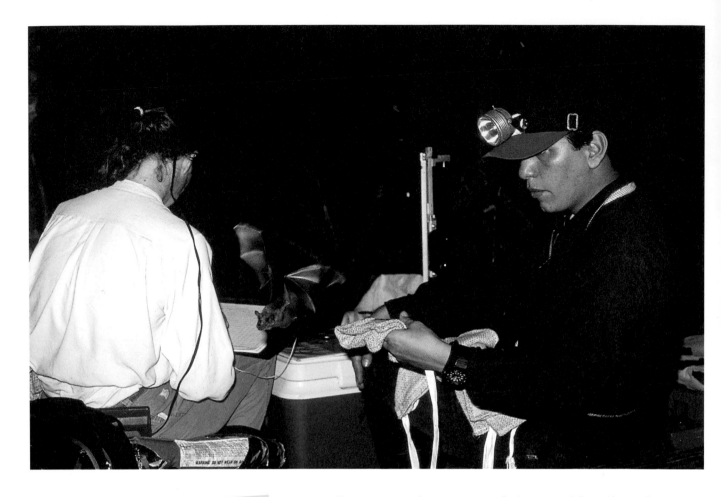

After Ceinwen Edwards marks the bat, José Rincon sets it free. If it is a large bat, it can be released at the research site. If it is a small bat, it is carried back to the place where it was captured. Small bats tend to fly in very small areas each night. A little bat might not be able to find its way back on its own.

Bat researchers around the world collect data in the same way. This allows them to compare bat populations in places that are far apart.

Back in the laboratory, Dietrich adds data from the last evening's research to the computer. Now he can compare each bat that he and the other researchers examined with other bats of the same species. This includes bats collected in the same place and those collected in other places. If a bat has been captured before, Dietrich will look to see how far it has traveled to reach the new place.

A Gathering of Guilds

Bat researchers on Barro Colorado Island have divided the bats they study into ten **guilds,** or groups. Guilds help researchers compare the different bats. The guilds are based on the kinds of food the bats eat, where they look for their food, and how they collect or catch it.

Because bats in the same guild act like each other, they often look very much alike. "Bats that fly closer to the dense forest have a wing shape that allows them to make tight turns," says Dietrich. "Other bats, the ones that fly in the open, have longer and narrower wings. They are very good at high speed, but they cannot make tight turns very well."

Studying the bodies of different bats helps researchers understand how each is built to live in its niche. "Look at the faces of the animals," says Dietrich. "Look at the different shapes. These differences reflect the place in which the bat lives and how it feeds."

Dietrich's work helps him compare the bats of Barro Colorado Island with bats in the larger mainland forest. There are fewer species on Barro Colorado Island. Dietrich wonders if this is because water separates the island from the mainland. He also wonders whether the number of bats living on the island changes in the same way on the mainland. And do bats move between the two places? Dietrich thinks that being separated from the mainland doesn't affect the bats very much. But more research is needed to find definite answers.

Compare the wing shapes of two bats that live very different lives. The Great Stripe-faced Bat (top) has short, fairly wide wings. These wings help it make tight turns in the thick forest where it finds its food. The Greater Bulldog Bat (bottom) flies across water to catch fish and insects. Its long, narrow wings help it travel far and fast.

The Bat Guilds of Barro Colorado Island

As part of a study of bats on Barro Colorado Island, researchers divided the 70 species found there into ten different guilds. The bats were grouped according to the places where they look for food, the types of food they eat, and how they collect or capture their food.

Guild ❶
Bats that look for insects in open areas and catch them while flying

Guild ❷
Bats that hunt for insects at forest edges and gaps

Guild ❸
Bats that hunt for insects in the air while flying in the thick forest

Guild ❹
Bats that eat large insects picked up from the ground and other surfaces

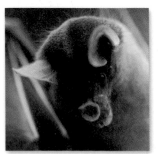

Guild ❺
Bats that eat small animals, such as birds, rodents, and even other bats found in the forest

Guild ❻
Bats that eat fish and some insects

Guild ❼
Bats that live only on blood

Guild ❽
Bats that eat fruit that is gathered in the forest or in shrubby areas

Guild ❾
Bats that mostly drink flower nectar that is collected in the forest or in shrubby areas

Guild ❿
Bats that eat anything they can find, including fruit, nectar, insects, and small animals

3 Getting to Know You

The bat cage is made of two small, wire rooms, each 4 by 4 meters (13 by 13 feet). The cage is covered by a roof, so researchers can work even when it rains.

Many bat studies on Barro Colorado Island are designed to find out which bats live where. But there are also many studies to learn more about just one or two species. In this type of study, a researcher wants to learn about a bat's life. This includes how the bat finds food, what it eats, and how much food it needs. Researchers sometimes use mist nets to capture a few bats from a species. These bats may then be taken to an outdoor laboratory that researchers call the "bat cage."

Elisabeth Kalko has taken part in bat cage studies with many kinds of bats. In one study, she and researcher Carmi Korine wanted to know how a group of fruit-eating bats called *Artibeus* found their food. They knew that the bats used echolocation to search for fruit. But they wondered how the bats found fruit hidden in leaves. Did the bats use other senses, such as smell? Elisabeth and Carmi did experiments with figs, one of this bat's favorite foods, to find out.

"We wanted to know if the bats were finding the fruit by its shape, its smell, or some other way," says Elisabeth. "To test for shape, we tried wax fruit shaped like figs." The bats ignored the fake fruit. "We tried freeze-dried fruit, which has no smell." The bats ignored this fruit, too. Before the researchers were ready to use real figs, they found some interesting results.

"I had some figs in a plastic bag under the chair I was sitting on in the cage as I observed the bats," says Elisabeth. "A fruit bat was flying around my head and around my legs. At first, I wondered why this bat was circling around me all the time. Then it suddenly landed underneath my chair. When I looked down, I saw that it had landed on the bag with figs. It was looking and looking, snubbling around, trying to find the scent source." The bat found the fruit even though it was hidden in a plastic bag.

Elisabeth and other researchers have learned a great deal about the ways that fruit-eating bats, like this Jamaican Fruit Bat, find their meals. Ten different species of bats on Barro Colorado Island eat the fruit of fig trees, which can be found all year round.

(above)
Seba's Short-tailed Bat often eats the spiky fruit of the piper plant, a member of the pepper family.

(below)
The Chestnut Short-tailed Bat (top) looks like Seba's Short-tailed Bat (bottom). But the two bats have different diets and they do not roost in the same types of places.

From this experiment, researchers now know that *Artibeus* fruit bats use echolocation mainly to know where they are and what's around them. When these bats want to find figs, they use their sense of smell to locate the hidden fruit.

Live and Let Live

How do two kinds of bats that seem very similar live near each other without competing for food or a place to live? It was another bat mystery. Wibke Thies, one of Elisabeth's students, solved it.

Wibke studied two kinds of short-tailed, fruit-eating bats. They were Seba's Short-tailed Bat and the Chestnut Short-tailed Bat. Their bodies look alike, but the Seba's Short-tailed Bat is just a little larger than the Chestnut Short-tailed Bat. Wibke wondered if

this size difference had to do with how far each bat traveled and the kinds of food each ate.

To study the bats, Wibke caught some in mist nets. She used glue that wears off after a few days to put a small radio transmitter on each bat. Then she set the bats free. Wibke and her assistants used equipment to listen for signals from the transmitters. As soon as they found a signal, they used it to follow the bat.

The transmitter made a slow pulsing sound when the bat was still, and a fast one when it was flying. With these signals Wibke and her assistants could tell if the bat was resting or if it was flying.

Wibke studied the two kinds of bats for several years. She studied the plants whose fruits these bats ate. She noticed where the plants grew and how much fruit they produced. She studied the seeds in the droppings of both species of bats. She also ran food experiments in the bat cage. In these experiments, bats could choose to eat the fruit they liked most.

Her results showed that the two kinds of bats, which seemed so alike at first, gather food very differently. Just as Wibke thought, the smaller species, the Chestnut Short-tailed Bat, looks for food in a small area. The larger species, Seba's Short-tailed Bat, looks for food in a wider area.

They eat different fruits, too. The Chestnut Short-tailed Bat mostly eats the fruit of piper plants, a plant related to the pepper plant. Different types of pipers grow their fruit at different times during the year. This means the Chestnut Short-tailed Bat has a steady diet.

Different Calls

Wibke is shown here doing field research. In the picture at the bottom of the page, she attaches a radio transmitter to the back of one of the bats she studied, the Chestnut Short-tailed Bat.

She learned that the Chestnut and Seba's Short-tailed Bats have different echolocation calls. The smaller Chestnut Short-tailed Bat makes shorter, higher-pitched calls than the larger Seba's Short-tailed Bat. This may be because the bats are different sizes. Wibke also learned that both types of bats rely on scent to help them find a meal in forest areas where fruit grows.

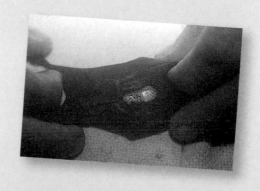

Seba's Short-tailed Bat eats the fruit of pipers and many other kinds of plants. But it eats fruit from only a few kinds of pipers. Because the two kinds of bats have different feeding habits, there is enough fruit for both of them.

Wibke also found out that the bats don't compete for housing on Barro Colorado Island. The larger species roosts in hollow trees. The smaller one lives beneath riverbanks and in the spaces between roots on the forest floor.

Wibke's study shows that two kinds of bats that seem to compete for the same food or housing don't. They each stay in their own niche. Because they are in different niches, these kinds of bats can live side by side.

Elisabeth Kalko is shown carrying an antenna. It is used to hear signals from a transmitter attached to a bat. The box at her waist lets her raise and lower the volume of the sounds she hears.

Peek-a-Boo

Discoveries often happen by accident. Elisabeth and another researcher wanted to study a frog-eating bat called *Trachops cirrhosus*, the Fringe-lipped Bat. Their plan was to attach a radio transmitter to the bat and track it, or follow it. But they couldn't catch one. Instead they put the transmitter on a *Tonatia*, or Round-eared Bat.

Usually a bat isn't tracked the first night that it wears a transmitter. "The bat might be irritated that night," Elisabeth explains. A bat may take a night to recover from being handled by humans. The next night, the researchers picked up a clear signal. This told them that the transmitter, hopefully still on the bat, was somewhere nearby. But something was strange. The signal wasn't moving. "It was already night, night, night!" remembers Elisabeth. The bat should have been out hunting.

Had the transmitter fallen off? "We had no idea where to look," says Elisabeth. "We really plowed through the leaves and looked everywhere." The researchers were under a tree that held a huge termite nest. "Just by chance, I moved the receiver a little bit," says Elisabeth. "I thought that the sound was coming from above and not from the ground." She was wearing a headlamp and looked up, right into the nest. "I saw that there was a hole in the termite nest. I saw a yellow flash. It was reflective tape on the transmitter. Wow! I found the bat!" The bat was living inside the termite nest—and it wasn't alone. It was crowded with about 20 other *Tonatias*. The termites didn't seem to mind sharing their space with these strange roommates.

It was a lucky find. Says Elisabeth, "We now know that the bats themselves hollow the termite nest and make their home in it. That is truly amazing. Up to now the only bats known to make their own homes were some fruit-eating bats. They make temporary homes inside large leaves by folding them to make tents. Then they hang under the tents."

Researchers found bats in a termite nest and made video films of their lives. "It is beautiful to watch them raise their families in there," says Elisabeth. The researchers are now working to find out how many termite nests on the island are home to bats.

4 Balance in Nature

When a bat catches insects for food, it seems like everything happens in fast motion. A bat can detect an insect, close in, and capture it in just a second. To survive, insects must hear bats coming in time to escape or have another way to avoid being eaten. The picture above shows a bat capturing an insect. The bat's image was recorded many times on a single photograph to show its flight path.

Bats are very good at finding food. They move quickly, they have powerful senses, and they are smart. Most often, insect-eating and frog-eating bats that go hunting for a meal find one. But if these bats caught everything they hunted, soon they wouldn't have enough to eat. Bats catch what they need, but enough prey get away to reproduce.

Scientists who study the insects and frogs that bats like to eat have noticed that prey sometimes act differently when bats are around. For example, some moths have ears that can hear bat calls as the bats approach. These moths may fly in unexpected patterns when they hear a bat approaching. Other moths send out a clicking sound that warns the bats that they taste terrible or are poisonous.

You Can't Catch Me

Katydids are large, slow-moving insects that look like grasshoppers. They are the favorite food of several kinds of tropical bats. About 100 different kinds of katydids have been found on Barro Colorado Island. They can be heard calling throughout the night.

Making and hearing sounds are important parts of katydids' lives. They are active at night. Because they can't see one another, katydids make sounds to say, "I am here!" or "This is my territory!" or "I am looking for a mate!" This last call is probably the most important sound of all. If the male katydid could not call to the female katydid, it would be hard for them to find each other. They wouldn't be able to reproduce. But these same sounds can spell doom for a katydid if they are heard by a hungry bat. Some bats use the sounds to find a katydid meal.

Jackie Belwood is a researcher at the Ohio Biological Survey and a scientist-in-residence at the Cincinnati Nature Center. She once spent two years on Barro Colorado Island. She studied katydids and the bats that eat them. Most of the time she studied the Round-eared Bat, the same kind of bat that Elisabeth Kalko found living in the termite nest.

(above)
Some moths, like this one, can hear bats approaching and may move away just in time.

(below)
Katydids are active at night, just like the bats who prey on them. Some katydids disguise their calls to hide from hunting bats.

Jackie compared the calls of two kinds of katydids. One kind lives in open fields away from **predators**, such as the Round-eared Bat. The other kind lives in the forest near predators. She found that katydids in open fields have different calls from katydids in the forest.

She says that male katydids that live in open fields sound like "tiny chain saws." They make loud, raspy calls for several minutes at a time. They call on and off for hours. Insects like these are easy to find. Even human researchers, who don't have bats' special hearing, can hear them.

Katydids that live in the dense forest have very different calls. Their calls sound like whistles. And they don't call for minutes at a time. They sing only once or twice a minute, for less than a second each time. They are almost impossible for a human to locate. And they are nearly as hard for a bat to find.

Jackie caught a Round-eared Bat and put it in the bat cage. Then she put two kinds of katydids in

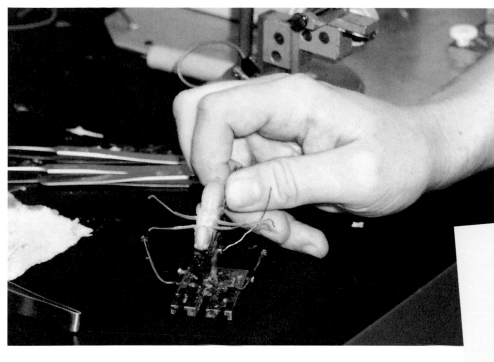

(above)
Electrical equipment can help researchers understand how the hearing system of the katydid takes in sounds.

(below)
Tonatia silvicola, the Round-eared Bat, has very long and sensitive ears. These ears help it hear the call of a single katydid.

the bat cage. One katydid made the chain saw call, and one made the whistle call. It took the bat just 26 seconds to locate the katydid that made the chain saw call. But it took more than 34 *minutes* for the bat to find the katydid that made the whistle call. Jackie concluded that over time, the call of the forest katydids changed. This change helped them survive.

It's harder for bats to find forest katydids, but bats do find them. Otherwise, there would be so many katydids in the forest that there wouldn't be enough food for all of them to eat. Just enough of the katydids are found by the bats to keep a balance between the predators and their prey.

Safety in Numbers

Like the katydid, the tungara frog is often heard at night in the Barro Colorado forest. It has a two-part call, known as the "whine" and the "chuck." The whine is loud, but it's hard to tell where it's coming from. The chuck part of its call makes the frog easy to find.

The male tungara frog uses the chuck call to let females know where it is. The chuck call can also tell frog-eating bats where to find a meal.

Tungara frogs seem to have developed a way to hide from frog-eating bats. Researchers have noticed that when male tungara frogs are alone or when there are just a few of them, they use mostly their whine call. But when there are many frogs, any one frog is less likely to be found by a bat. The frogs then use both the whine and the chuck calls.

Sometimes there are too many katydids or too many bats in one place. If there are too many katydids, some of them might not survive because they can't find enough to eat. If there are too many bats, some bats might leave to go to another place where there are plenty of katydids to eat. Nature almost always finds a way to strike a balance.

Come Here, You Bat, You!

Bats help some members of the rain forest, including plants. Some bats drink the nectar inside flowers that bloom at night. The snouts of nectar-feeding bats are long and thin. Their tongues can reach deep inside the flowers to lap up nectar. Usually some pollen, or tiny grains that make it possible for flowers to reproduce, from inside the flower sticks to the bats' fur.

When the bats travel to the next flower, the pollen they are "wearing" is carried along. The pollen can join with cells in the next flower. This allows the plant to reproduce, or make new plants. These bats help night-blooming flowers in the same way that bees, butterflies, hummingbirds, and other animals help flowers that bloom during the day.

Many bats also help spread fruit seeds. When a bat gathers fruit, it usually carries it some distance. The bat goes to a feeding roost to eat. Sometimes the bat spits out the seeds as it eats. Other times the seeds pass through the bat's digestive system whole, because the bats don't chew the seeds. The seeds fall to the ground as part of the bat's droppings. In this way bats "spray" seeds over large areas as they fly.

If conditions are right, the seeds sprayed by the bats begin to grow. It is easier for seeds to grow away from the parent plant. The distance between the seeds means they don't compete for water or

light. Also, the small plant is less likely to be attacked by a disease if it is far from the parent plant. "The seeds grow better far away," says Elisabeth Kalko.

Bats may carry seeds several kilometers (more than a mile) from the original tree. "Bats carry the fruit to places where the seeds have a fair chance to start to grow," Elisabeth says. By aiding pollination and by carrying seeds to good growing places, bats help the rain forest.

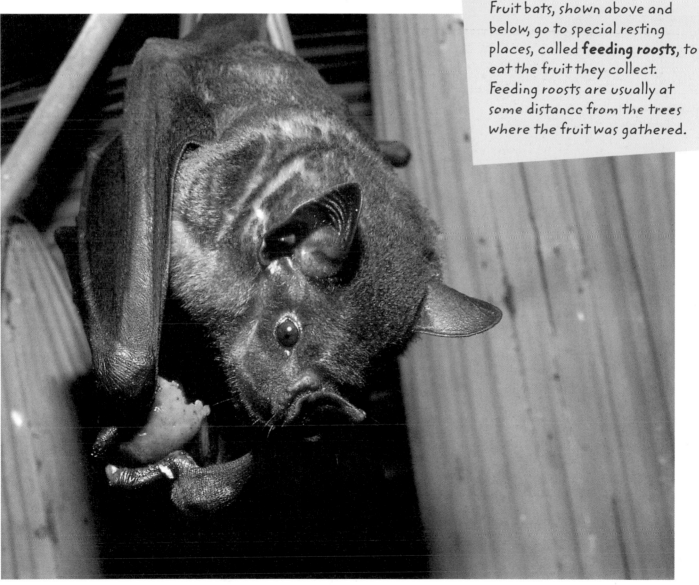

Fruit bats, shown above and below, go to special resting places, called **feeding roosts**, to eat the fruit they collect. Feeding roosts are usually at some distance from the trees where the fruit was gathered.

5 Other Forests, Other Labs

Barro Colorado Island (above) is a great place to do rain forest research. The forest is crowded with a huge number of different species. It is completely protected, so it is not in danger of being destroyed or changed.

Researchers on Barro Colorado Island know that the forest they are studying will stay untouched. Game wardens keep watch night and day. They protect the island from people who might harm the plants or animals. People may come to the island to visit, but their numbers are controlled. It is a safe place for rain forest plants and animals. Here, scientists can create a picture of how the plants and animals in a rain forest community live together. They don't have to worry that the forest might one day be destroyed.

But this is not the case in other parts of the world. Rain forests are cut down for lumber, or to make room for cattle, or to raise crops. Mining or oil operations sometimes destroy the natural forest. People who want to protect rain forests often work closely with governments and local people. They try to find ways to help people who live in or near rain forests earn a living without harming the rain forest.

Batting in Brazil

In addition to working on Barro Colorado Island, Elisabeth Kalko works in the Amazon rain forest north of Manaus, Brazil. She also works in an African country called Ivory Coast. These are only two of the many places in the world where rain forests are threatened. In Brazil Elisabeth works with student Erica Sampaio and Charles Handley of the National Museum of Natural History in Washington, D.C. Dr. Handley took part in the first studies of bats on Barro Colorado Island.

This is a forest study site near Manaus, Brazil. While some tall trees still survive, much forest land has been cleared. Researchers want to know what types of rain forest species are able to survive in the forest areas that remain.

The researchers in Brazil want to know how much diversity, or variety of species, can be maintained in a small forest plot. They also want to compare the forest plots to undisturbed forest.

Manaus

The False Vampire Bat, shown below, is one species being studied at the site in Brazil.

In Brazil, large sections of forest have been cut down to make room for cattle. The World Wildlife Fund, the Smithsonian Institution, the Brazilian government, and cattle owners agreed to preserve squares of forest in and around cattle grazing land. These plots of land are called "**forest fragments**."

Scientists are studying these forest fragments to find out how many animals and plants can live on small plots of forest. They also wonder if plants or animals move back and forth between the large, undisturbed rain forest areas and the forest fragments. "One of the goals of this project is to find out which plants and animals can do this and which can't," says Elisabeth.

The bat researchers count how many species of bats they find living on the smallest fragments. Then they compare this number with the number of species found in larger fragments and in the nearby undisturbed forests. This tells researchers how many kinds of bats can live in forest fragments.

Many of the same tools used by researchers on

Barro Colorado Island are used in Brazil. These include mist nets, multiflash cameras, and especially the bat detector. The bat detector has made it possible to count many kinds of bats that fly too high to be caught in mist nets. Without this tool, bat counts would be much less complete.

As each study is finished, the results are shared with other research groups. Researchers are learning how well forest fragments can support all the different kinds of rain forest life.

Understanding the Results

Researchers have found that there are fewer species of animals and plants in the forest fragments than in large, undisturbed rain forest areas. And conditions in the forests are different.

Wind damages the plants at the edges of the fragments. So the kinds of plants that grow in forest fragments are different from those that grow in the large, undisturbed forest. Some trees that grow well in undisturbed rain forests can't live in the fragments. Other plants that do poorly in the heart of a forest do well in a fragment. The plants in each environment attract different kinds of animals.

But while a small forest fragment may be home to fewer species of plants or animals, many can still survive. For instance, fruit-eating bats that feed on shrubs, or small bushes, do well in forest fragments.

Here, Elisabeth uses a bat detector to collect sounds in the night forest.

This flying fox, called a Hammerhead Bat, is one of the animals being studied by researchers in Taï National Park.

Researchers have also studied forest fragments that are connected to the large forest by shrubs and small trees. Here, they found many different kinds of bats. "That suggests that the shrubs and trees are used by bats to move back and forth between forest fragments and the larger forest," says Elisabeth.

These findings suggest ways to manage the use of land. If land is managed well, then there will be enough room for cattle to graze and enough forest for bats, other animals, and plants.

The work in Brazil has helped create a new field of science. It is called "**restoration ecology.**" Elisabeth and others hope that people who go into this new field will be able to work with other scientists and government officials. Perhaps together they can make good decisions about how to preserve all the different species in tropical forests. And they can help find ways for the people who live nearby to earn their living.

Into Africa

Elisabeth is doing similar work in Ivory Coast, Africa. There she is working with Jakob Fahr. Jakob is an expert on bats in that region. "The sad truth is that people in western Africa fight for their existence," says Elisabeth. "They need land to grow food for survival. They hunt in the rain forest to get meat for their families."

Better farming methods can make it possible to grow more food on less land. This would mean that less rain forest would need to be cut down for farming. But threats to this forest come from other places, too. "Most of the forest in Ivory Coast has been cleared by logging companies due to the high demand for wood in western Africa, the United States, Europe, and Asia," Elisabeth says.

There are a few national parks in western Africa where the forest is protected. The Taï National Park is one. It is an important reserve because it is the only large area of tropical lowland forest left in Ivory Coast. It is also where Elisabeth and Jakob study African bats. "In western Africa, the forests are vanishing particularly quickly," says Elisabeth. "Especially rain forests. And one of our goals in the tropics right now is to understand the role that bats play in helping the forest restore itself—before it is too late."

Time is running out. "I just returned from Ivory Coast," says Elisabeth. "There are incredibly large areas of forest that have already been cut down." There is no way to know what it used to be like and what used to live there. "An animal that can only live in the rain forest would never be able to survive there today."

Still, Elisabeth is hopeful. She works tirelessly to learn about bats and the rain forests where they live. She is glad for every chance she has to tell people about what she learns. "I think right now there is a great interest in rain forests," she says.

Elisabeth wants us to appreciate rain forests and to know how necessary it is to preserve them. She is joined by many other people around the world who are dedicated to studying and preserving these special places.

The loss of rain forests is a serious problem in many poor countries. Some people cut down forests as a way to help save themselves from hunger or poverty.

This chimpanzee lives safely in Taï National Park. But nearby forests are in danger of destruction.

Glossary

bat detector A device that researchers use to listen to the high-pitched calls of bats. The bat detector makes bat calls sound lower, and in some cases slower. This helps scientists identify the bats they observe.

capture bag A soft fabric bag. Researchers use the bag to hold individual bats until the bats can be examined and released.

community A group of organisms sharing an environment.

data recorder A person who writes down information about the bats that are examined at a research site.

echolocate A method bats and some other animals use to find their way in the dark, and in some cases, to hunt for food. The bats make high-pitched calls that bounce off objects.

feeding roosts Branches, ledges, leaves, and other spots where some bats perch to eat.

forest fragments Pieces of forest left in open land that has been cleared for logging, farming, or cattle grazing.

guild A group of bats that are alike in many ways. They find, gather, and eat similar kinds of food. There are ten bat guilds on Barro Colorado Island and the nearby mainland forests.

isthmus [ISS-muss] A narrow strip of land that connects two larger bodies of land.

mammal A warm-blooded animal that gives birth to live young that are fed with milk.

mist net A lightweight net strung between poles. The nets are used to capture bats so they can be studied by researchers.

multiflash camera system A system of two cameras attached to 12 electronic flashes. The shutters of both cameras stay open while the flashes go off very quickly, one after another. Each picture the system takes is many pictures in one. Bat researchers use the system to take pictures of flying bats.

nature reserve An area where all plants and animals are strictly protected.

niche [NITCH] Where a species lives, how it gathers food, and its role in the community.

night vision scope Special binoculars that make light seem many times brighter.

Panama A Central American country located south of Costa Rica and north of Colombia. Panama has coastlines on both the Atlantic and Pacific oceans. A narrow channel called the Panama Canal was dug nearly 100 years ago across the Isthmus of Panama. The canal connects the oceans.

predator An animal that hunts for and eats other animals.

prey Food hunted by a predator.

rain forest A very wet forest.

research site A location for projects, such as the site where researchers gather information about bats using mist nets, bat detectors, or multiflash systems.

restoration ecology A field of science in which researchers work, often with government officials and local people, to try to restore land.

species A group of plants or animals able to breed with one another and create offspring that can reproduce.

terminal buzz A set of very fast calls that bats make just before they try to capture prey.

wingspan The length of an animal's wings, from the tip of one outstretched wing to the tip of the other.

Further Reading

Ackerman, Diane, and Merlin Tuttle (Photographer). *Bats: Shadows in the Night.* New York: Crown, 1997.

Bernard, Robin. *Bats: Complete Cross-Curricular Theme Unit That Teaches About This Amazing Mammal.* New York: Scholastic Trade, 1998.

Graham, Gary L., and Fiona A. Reid (Illustrator). *Bats of the World: 103 Species in Full Color (A Golden Guide).* New York: Golden Books Publishing Company, 1994.

Jennings, Jane F. G. *Bats: A Creativity Book for Young Conservationists.* Austin, TX: University of Texas Press, 1996.

Wilson, Don E., and Merlin D. Tuttle (Photographer). *Bats in Question: The Smithsonian Answer Book.* Washington: Smithsonian Institution, 1996.

Index

Acknowledgments

Thanks above all to Dr. Elisabeth Kalko, formerly of the University of Tübingen, Germany, and more recently of the University of Ulm, Germany, and the Smithsonian Institution. Elisabeth has done all she can to support this project from its inception. I'm thankful for the time, advice, and insights she has contributed. It has been a privilege to collaborate with her on this project.

I'm also very grateful to Dietrich von Staden, a graduate student in the Department of Animal Physiology at the University of Tübingen, Germany. He introduced me to Barro Colorado Island and the scientists working there. He has also offered thoughtful and helpful comments throughout the book's development.

Elisabeth and Dietrich were instrumental in assembling, and in many instances, photographing, the fantastic images of bats and bat research that bring the book to life. I appreciate this, and also the efforts of the other photographers, particularly Dietmar Nill.

Georgina de Alba, Education Director of the Smithsonian Tropical Research Institute of Panama City, Panama, her assistant, Adriana Bilgray, and Oris Acevedo, Science Coordinator of Barro Colorado Island, were all very helpful and cooperative.

Wibke Thies, Jacqueline Belwood, Erica Sampaio, and Jakob Fahr kindly reviewed portions of the text pertaining to their research. Alex Lange and Ingeborg Teppner, graduate students at the University of Graz, Austria, shared background on current katydid research.

Patricia Wynne, a colleague of many years, delighted me with her drawings and her endless enthusiasm and dedication.

Elisabeth wishes to acknowledge Dr. Charles Handley of the National Museum of Natural History (Smithsonian Institution) in Washington, D.C. She notes, "It is thanks to his fabulous knowledge and enthusiasm that I became interested in tropical bats." She also acknowledges Professor Hans-Ulrich Schnitzler of the University of Tübingen in Germany, "who has helped me to develop and stay in the 'bat' career. Much of the fascinating equipment we use has been developed thanks to his continuous support, help, and ideas."

Animals, Animals/Lepine, Francis: 4 main image; Animals, Animals/Murray, Bertram G. Jr.: 33 top; Animals, Animals/Richards, M.: 43; Fahr, Jakob: 42; Kaipf, Ingrid: 12 top and middle, 20 upper right, 41; Kalko, Elisabeth: 11 top, 12 bottom, 14, 16 main image, 18 upper left, 23, 24 bottom, 26 main image, 27, 31, 32 main image, 39, 40; Kovacs, Deborah: 34, 35 bottom; Krull, Dorothea: 30; Lee, Dr. Julian C.: 36 bottom; Molinari, Jesús: 8 spot, 11 bottom, 25 top; Nill, Dietmar: cover, 1, 3 top, 4 upper right, 5 top, 7, 8 main image, 10, 13, 16 upper right, 19 bottom, 26 upper right, 28 top, 32 upper right, 36 top, 37 top, 38 upper right; Thies, Wibke: 29; von Staden, Dietrich: 1, 2, 3 bottom, 5 bottom, 9, 15, 17, 18 bottom, 19 top, 20 middle and bottom, 21, 22, 24 top four images, 25 bottom four images, 28 middle and bottom, 33 bottom, 35 top, 37 bottom, 38 main image.

Illustrations on page 6 are by David Stevenson. Illustrations on pages 14–15 and 24–25 are by Patricia Wynne. Illustrations on pages 40 and 43 are by Jill Leichter.